ALL YOU NEED TO KNOW ABOUT

Herbs and

Spices

by

G.B. WOODIN

Nutmeg

PETER PAUPER PRESS, INC.
WHITE PLAINS • NEW YORK

INTRODUCTION

THERE has yet to be a palatable dish without some sort of seasoning. In consequence, if you aspire to be a good cook, you should know your herbs and spices, the main flavor source of the world's greatest cookery.

Put your trust in Persephone, the goddess of all that grows. Herbs (the leaves of plants grown in the temperate zone) and spices (the barks, fruits, roots, and seeds of sundry plants indigenous to the tropics) will not change the chemistry of your cooking nor will they make it necessary for you to revise old stand-by recipes. The same holds true of aromatic seeds of herbaceous plants which grow in hot climates, mild climates, or both. In toto, such flora should be used to heighten rather than to hide the natural flavors of foods. The overall impression should be one of savoriness with no particular herb or spice omnipotent, excepting in the case of curry, chili, and gingerbread, where the character of the dish depends on its spiciness.

Experience is a noble teacher. Feel free to experiment, but be ever mindful of the golden mean. A subtle dash of seasoning can be marvelous; a lot of it can be overpowering. There are no definite formulae, since some seasonings are delicate, while others are either pungent or hot. If a recipe is not available, try one-quarter teaspoon of herb or spice (less if it happens to be pepper or garlic) per pound of meat or pint of sauce, soup, or vegetable, and test for taste. Dried herbs are much stronger than fresh herbs, so that three or four times as much of the latter may be used.

Keep herbs and spices in airtight containers, away from heat. Exposure to heat and air robs them of their flavor and fragrance.

When buying herbs and spices, look first for rich, fresh color; then note the aroma. Except for non-aromatic or faintly fragrant items, such as dry (seed or powdered) mustard, poppy and sesame seeds, the pungency should rise to greet you, hale and hearty.

Besides telling you all you need to know about herbs and spices, this book will likewise introduce you to dehydrated vegetable seasonings such as celery, garlic, onion, etc. and blends such as curry powder, mixed pickling spice, poultry seasoning, etcetera.

To quote Shakespeare, "O! mickle is the powerful grace that lies in herbs. . . ."

ALL YOU NEED TO KNOW
ABOUT HERBS AND SPICES

HERBS & SPICES

ALLSPICE
(Pimenta officinalis)

THE allspice tree, a shiny-leaved evergreen plant of the myrtle family indigenous to Jamaica, Guatemala, Honduras, and Mexico, bears a brownish, peppercornish berry which tastes similar to cinnamon, cloves, and nutmeg combined. Sometimes confused with mixed pickling spice (a mixture of allspice berries and a dozen other spices), and sometimes called "pimento," allspice is used "whole" for meat broths, gravies, green pea soup, beef stew, boiled fish, and pickling liquids; and "ground" for meat loaf, baked ham, tomatoes, beets, spinach, squash, turnips, red cabbage, relishes, fruit cake, preserves, fruit compote, baked bananas, tapioca pudding, chocolate pudding, and all cranberry dishes.

ANISE SEED
(*Pimpinella anisum*)

A MEDICINE in ancient Egypt, a digestive at Caesarean feasts, and an amulet against bad dreams and the evil eye in the Middle Ages, this small, greenish-brown seed of an herbaceous plant of the parsley family is unmistakably identified by its "licorice" flavor and aroma. Grown mainly in Spain, Syria, and Turkey, anise is happily discovered in cookies, cakes, fruit compote, stewed apples, and fruit pie fillings. The Roman naturalist Pliny recommended it as an excellent spice for chicken, duck, and veal. Orange sherbet, dotted with anise, makes an ideal, easy-to-serve dessert. Anise is used in the making of Anisette, an Italian liqueur.

BASIL
(*Ocimum basilicum*)

THIS delightful herb, grown in the United States, France, Hungary, and Belgium, is a member of the mint family native to India and Iran. The Hindu ritualist plants it around his home to insure happiness; the Italian romanticist

8

Chervil

Cumin
Seed

Cardamom
Seed

Allspice

wears it to show he is in love; the French gour-
met calls it the *herbe royale*. Basil leaves, which
rival oregano as a seasoning for pizza, spaghetti,
and tomato dishes, add both flavor and fragrance to vegetable soups, meat pies, stews,
peas, zucchini, green beans, and cucumbers.
Carthusian monks, at Grenoble, France, use
basil in the making of Chartreuse, an aromatic
liqueur.

BAY LEAF
(*Laurus nobilis*)

THERE are more legends and superstitions as-
sociated with bay leaf than with almost any
other herb. To cite an instance: Daphne, a
beautiful nymph who saw fit to flee from Apol-
lo, the Greek god of sunlight, prophecy, music,
and poetry, was turned into an evergreen tree
(the sweet bay or laurel), whose leaves became
the symbol of victory and renown, honor and
scholarship. The word "baccalaureate" was de-
rived from laurel berries; the phrase "winning
your laurels" originally meant a wreath of lau-

rel (bay) leaves. Endemic to Greece, Portugal, and Yugoslavia, bay leaf is especially recommended for the seasoning of meats, potatoes, stews, soups, sauces, and fish.

CARAWAY SEED
(*Carum carvi*)

SOME two thousand years ago, the Romans did a land-office business in caraway seed, selling it to most of the civilized world. Medieval epicures fancied it in comfit, a dry sweetmeat containing nuts and fruit. North Europeans, especially the English and Germans, have long used this member of the parsley family as a seasoning. Kümmel, a German liqueur, is made with caraway seed. The plant, grown plenteously by Danes and Dutchmen, has a tendency to shatter when ripe, so it must be harvested at night or in the early morning while still covered with dew. The seed, which comes "whole" (as seen in rye bread, baked goods, and cheese), is used for pork and sauerkraut dishes, new cabbage, noodles, soups, and stews.

CARDAMOM SEED
(Elettaria cardamomum)

CARDAMOM, a member of the ginger family native to tropical Asia, is the world's second most precious spice plant, yielding no more than two hundred and fifty pounds of pods per acre. The pods, each containing from fifteen to twenty tiny aromatic seeds, must be snipped from plants with scissors, a tedious task. Cardamom seed is available either in the pod or decorticated (outer pod removed) and can be either "whole" or "ground." Use it sparingly in pastry, apple and pumpkin pies, grape jelly, and curry.

CELERY SEED
(Apium graveolens)

THE fruit of a plant of the parsley family which grows prodigiously in France and India, celery seed was originally used for medicinal purposes and copiously covered in writings by Homer, the Greek poet, who wrote the *Iliad* and the *Odyssey*. The smallish, olive-brown seed (it takes 750,000 or more to make one pound) has a parsley-nutmeg flavor and is packaged "whole" or as celery salt, a mixture of celery seed and salt. Either variety is excellent in soups, tomato juice, oyster stew, clam chowder, clam juice, salad dressings, braised lettuce, eggs, chicken croquettes, and canapé mixtures.

CHERVIL
(*Anthriscus cerefolium*)

NATIVE to eastern Europe and an ally of parsley, chervil is unlike many other herbaceous plants, standing completely free from folklore and uses in medicine and magic. Its lacy, fern-like leaves, often used as an alternative to parsley, are pleasantly aromatic and strongly suggestive of tarragon, another famous herb. Chervil is often included in a famous blend called *les fines herbes* and lends both flavor and fragrance to salads, stuffings, sauces, and omelets.

CHIVE
(*Allium Schoenoprasum*)

USED by Roman cooks before Christ, chive is undoubtedly one of the most favored of seasonings. A small, bulbous plant, closely related to the onion and leek, chive thrives in the United States, giving off long, slender, green leaves which grow back like grass when sheared regularly. Available in a freeze-dried form for convenient spice-shelf storage, chive adds zestfulness to vichyssoise, cream-dressed baked potatoes, vegetables, salads, sauces, gravies, dips, cheese and egg dishes.

CINNAMON
(Cinnamomum cassia)

CINNAMON, one of the first seasonings and the most important baking spice, has been used not only for flavoring but for medicine, perfume, and incense. Egyptian pharaohs fancied it as a love potion; Roman emperors called for it in their baths. This pungently sweet spice, the inner bark of lauraceous (laurel) evergreen trees, comes in two different types: The popular, robust East Indian variety (sometimes called "cassia"), which is reddish brown in color, and the less-popular Ceylonese, which is pale tan. Ground cinnamon goes well in cakes, buns, breads, cookies, mashed sweet potatoes, hot chocolate, and chocolate desserts. A bit of whole-stick cinnamon does wonders for beef stew, and is delicious as a flavoring for hot cider.

CLOVE
(Eugenia aromatica)

THE clove, a tropical myrtaceous (myrtle) tree growing on the coasts of Madagascar and Tanzania, gives forth with a nail-like bud which was once the cause of wars and an anathema to many European traders. Considered costly centuries ago (upwards of 7,000 dried clove buds are needed to make one pound), clove is now readily available "whole" for use in studding ham and pork, and "ground" for use in stews, gravies, beets, sweet potatoes, winter squash, baked goods, chocolate mixtures and desserts, spicy sweet syrups, and pickled fruits.

CORIANDER SEED
(Coriandrum sativum)

OUTSTANDING among the flora of the Mediterranean, the coriander plant is deeply rooted in

Oregano

Turmeric

Coriander
Seed

Paprika

history. Its seed was discovered in early Egyptian tombs; its fragrance enriched the Hanging Gardens of Babylon; its flavor was compared to that of manna by ancient Hebrews. The seed of this herbaceous plant of the parsley family is found in candies and in the ever-popular frankfurter. It is used "whole" in mixed pickles, gingerbread, cookies, biscuits, poultry stuffing, and mixed green salad. Rub ground coriander on fresh pork before roasting.

CUMIN SEED
(Cuminum cyminum)

THIS seed, coming from a small plant resembling celery or parsley, was used by the Pharisees to pay tithes and by English vassals to pay quitrents in lieu of feudal services. Sometimes spelled "cummin" and sometimes called "comino seed," cumin undeniably suggests its kinship with caraway, in both appearance and aroma. Exported by Iran, Lebanon, Morocco, and Syria, cumin seed is one of the chief ingredients in chili and curry powders. German cooks add it to pork and sauerkraut; the Dutch and Swiss use it in cheese. Try it "whole" or "ground" in soups, pies, and stuffed eggs; for a tempting canapé, mix chutney with snappy cheese and garnish with cumin seed.

DILL SEED
(*Anethum graveolens*)

A NOTED member of the parsley family and a popular potherb, dill was once sold by apothecaries "to calm nervous stomachs and to hinder witches of their will." Native to Europe and cultivated to some extent in the United States, dill seed is essential in the making of dill pickles and excellent in meats, fish, sauces, coleslaw, potato salad, macaroni, and sauerkraut; dill weed (the leaf of the plant) is especially suited to salads, sandwich fillings, and boiled fish dishes.

FENNEL SEED
(*Foeniculum vulgare*)

IT was on a field of fennel that the Greeks defeated the Persians in the Battle of Marathon (490 B. C.). Hence, "marathon" became the

Greek word for "fennel." Fennel, a perennial umbelliferous (carrot-like) plant found in Europe, India, and Argentina, was long viewed as one of the nine sacred herbs which counteracted the nine causes of disease. The seed, somewhat like anise, is highly popular in bread, rolls, apple pie, seafood, pork and poultry dishes. It is fennel that gives Italian sausage its characteristic flavor.

FENUGREEK SEED
(Trigonella foenum-graecum)

ONCE prized for its medicinal properties, this seed from a plant of the pea family was prescribed by early physicians to encourage digestive processes and to discourage fevers. It still appears in the *U. S. Pharmacopoeia* as an important ingredient in laxatives. Imported from India, France, Lebanon, and Argentina, this tiny, reddish-brown seed has a pleasantly bitter flavor suggestive of curry powder in which it plays an important role. It is used mainly for the making of chutney and imitation maple flavoring.

GINGER
(*Zingiber officinale*)

INDIGENOUS to the East Indies and introduced to the Antilles by Spanish explorers shortly after the discovery of the New World, ginger was considered for centuries as the rich man's spice, rivalling popular black pepper in price. The root, or rhizome, of a reedlike perennial plant, ginger comes "whole" for use in chutneys, conserves, syrups, and pickling vinegar, and "ground" for use in gingerbread, cakes, pumpkin pie, Indian pudding, canned fruits, roasts, and other meats. Crystallized or preserved ginger is considered a confection, not a spice. Try rubbing a chicken, inside and out, with a mixture of ginger and butter before roasting.

MARJORAM
(*Majorana hortensis*)

CREATED by Venus to heal a wound caused by one of Cupid's darts, marjoram became the symbol of love and was used for ages in medicines and perfumes. The French used it to make "hippocras," an elaborate spiced wine. Native

Ginger

Pepper

Fennel
Seed

Basil

to western Asia and the Mediterranean area and cultivated in the United States, marjoram is sold "whole" or "ground" to heighten the flavor of lima beans, peas, and green beans, and is one of the herbs used in poultry seasoning. Sprinkle it over lamb while cooking.

MINT
(Mentha piperita and Mentha spicata)

THERE are as many varieties of mint as there are sparks from Vulcan's furnace, says an anonymous, ninth-century writer. The number of uses for mint in the Middle Ages was almost equal to the number of species. *Banckes's Herbal*, printed in 1525, describes how, rubbed on the teeth, mint will give "a sweet-smelling mouth"; made into a sauce, "it will make thee to have a talent (appetite) to try thy meat"; used as a poultice, "it will cure blotches on the face." Herbalist Gerarde writes "it was crushed and rubbed on table tops . . . and strewn in chambers and places of recreation, pleasure, and repose." Religious Frenchmen referred reverently to the herb as "Our Lady's Mint." Ancient cookbooks, replete with herbal recipes, lauded the use of mint in meat dishes, salads, and omelets. Mint—more specifically, peppermint and spearmint—is today cultivated in the United States as well as in Europe and finds wide use in soups, stews, fish dishes, peas, carrots, and beverages. Mint, sauce or jelly, is a "must" with lamb.

MUSTARD
(Brassica hirta and Brassica juncea)

NOVELIST Anatole France says in *The Revolt of the Angels*: "A tale without love is like beef without mustard: an insipid dish." An untold number of people must support this viewpoint toward mustard, consuming, as they do, more than 400-million pounds of it each year. Mustard, unlike other aromatic spices, has no aroma whatever, so long as it remains in a dry state. Its pungency rises only after it has been mixed with water, grape juice, or similar liquid. Raised in the United States and imported from Canada, Denmark, and the United Kingdom, mustard grows in two different types: *Brassica hirta* (white or yellow) and *Brassica juncea* which falls into two groupings, brown and Oriental. Besides prepared ("hot dog") mustard, there are "seed" for use in boiled beets, salads, and pickling meats, and "powdered" for use in meats, fish, fowl, sauces, salad dressings, cheese and egg dishes.

NUTMEG AND MACE
(*Myristica fragrans*)

ROMANY girls used nutmeg as a charm to hold their lovers. European merchants used to charge three sheep or half a cow for one pound of mace. The two spices, which come from the peach-like fruit of an evergreen tree native to Southeast Asia, are intimately related: nutmeg, the pit or seed of the fruit, and mace, the lacy tissue which covers it. The aroma of tan-colored nutmeg is sweeter and more delicate than that of orange-tinted mace. Nutmeg, available "whole" or "ground," is used in baked goods, puddings, sauces, chicken soup, butter for corn-on-the-cob and spinach, candied sweet potatoes, and eggnog. Mace, livelier and more pungent in flavor than nutmeg, is especially good in cherry pie, pound cake, gravies, and, believe it or not, in fish concoctions and meat stuffings.

OREGANO
(Origanum)

SOME two thousand years ago, the Greeks gave this herb of the mint family the poetic name of "joy of the mountain." It has since been called "wild marjoram," "winter sweet," "originy," and "origan." Closely related to, but spicier than marjoram, oregano has become very popular in the United States, largely because of the ever-growing appetite for pizza and other Italian specialties. Mediterranean oregano is distinctly different in character and flavor from the "Mexican sage" variety which is used in chili powder and Mexican foods. Sold "whole" or "ground," oregano adds a welcome flavor to meat, fish, cheese and egg dishes, tomatoes and zucchini.

PAPRIKA
(Capsicum annuum)

HUNGARIANS gave this spice its name, when they were introduced to it by the Turks in the sixteenth century. (Interesting to note, paprika did not originate in Turkey but in the Western Hemisphere.) The red pepper, whence comes paprika, varies from no pungency whatever to a slight bite. By far, the greatest proportion of paprika sold in the United States is sweet in taste and brilliantly red in color. Favored as a garnish, it can be used generously to give eye appeal to a wide variety of dishes, including salads, salad dressings, fish, meat and poultry, soups, eggs, and vegetables.

PARSLEY
(*Petroselinum crispum*)

ENDEMIC to the Mediterranean area and cultivated in the United States, parsley, according to a Shropshire proverb, must be sown nine times, for the devil takes all but the last. Juno, the queen of Roman gods, pastured her horses in a field of parsley to make them spirited. Ancient Greeks wore parsley crowns to achieve serenity and encourage their appetite. In *The Goodman of Paris*, a medieval cookbook, parsley was listed as an "essential" in omelets and green pickles. Even in those days it was used as a garnish. Dehydrated parsley flakes are usually sold in larger containers than other herbs, since they are used more freely. Essentially, parsley flakes should be added toward the end of the cooking period and be allowed to soak when used in salad dressings, dips, sandwich spreads, etc. Try adding parsley, along with onion salt and paprika, the next time you make potato cakes.

PEPPER, BLACK & WHITE
(*Piper nigrum*)

LONG viewed as "the master spice," pepper was once so precious that it was weighed out like gold and used as a medium of exchange. Rents, dowries, and taxes were paid in pepper. If Columbus had not managed to sell his financial backers on the idea that he could find a shorter route to this "spicy treasure" of the Orient, he would not have discovered the New World as he did. The American merchant marine would not have sailed as it did, if it had not been for the quest for pepper. Pepper, both black and white, comes from a vine, the berries of which grow like grapes. Black pepper is made from berries with the dark outer hull left on; white pepper, more popular in Europe than in the United States, is made from berries without the dark outer hull. Use whole pepper (peppercorns) in soups and stews, and ground pepper in meats, sauces, gravies, vegetables, salads, etc. White pepper goes well in light-colored dishes where dark specks are best unseen.

POPPY SEED
(Papaver somniferum)

THE poppy, whence come the flower, poppy seed, and opium, is native to the Mediterranean area, from which it was carried off by Islamic missionaries to the Far East. Have no qualms about the opium. The seed cannot form until after the plant has matured to a point where it has lost all of its potential as an opiate. Good cooks use it as a topping for rolls, bread, cakes, cookies, noodles, rice, green beans, boiled onions, and broiled fish.

Dill Seed

Mace

Thyme

Poppy Seed

RED PEPPER OR CAYENNE
(Capsicum frutescens)

SOUTH America is the ancestral home of the pod pepper (*Capsicum*) family, the source of red pepper or cayenne. Peter Martyr, a shipmate of Columbus, wrote: "There are innumerable kinds of *Ages* (the Indian name for pod pepper), the variety whereof is known by their leaves and flowers. In all shapes and sizes, some are red, some yellow, some violet, some brown, and some white. Here, at last, is pepper more pungent than that from Caucasus." The variety of hot peppers, as Martyr indicated, is almost unlimited. Undoubtedly, the most popular are ground red pepper, crushed red pepper, and cayenne. Red pepper, ground or crushed, is prepared from larger but less pungent pod peppers, all true red. Cayenne, characteristically an orange-colored spice, is prepared from the hottest pod peppers ("chilies"), varying from red to yellow in color. Although these categories are followed by most packagers, there are those who contend that ground red pepper and cayenne are the same — meaning a ground, very hot pepper. Actually, the matter of terminology makes little difference. Any one of these hot spices will produce the same spark of flavor. Indubitably, each should be used with a light hand. Generally speaking, ground red pepper or cayenne goes best in meats, sauces, eggs, fish, and vegetables; crushed red pepper — sometimes called pepperoni rosso, pizza pepper, or coarse crushed red pepper — adds piquancy to spaghetti, pizza, and other Latinic dishes.

ROSEMARY
(*Rosmarinus officinalis*)

IN the great sweep of the ages, this revered herb of the mint family has been treasured for many reasons, apart from its culinary uses. Brides carried rosemary as the symbol of fidelity; bridegrooms considered it as a good luck charm. The Christmas boar's head was garlanded with rosemary; the water for hand washing at table was scented with it. *Banckes's Herbal* says that if you "take the flowers and put them in a chest among your clothes or among books, the moths shall not hurt them. . . . Also, put the leaves

31

under thy bed's head and thou shalt be delivered of all evil dreams. . . ." Deriving its name from two Latin words which read "dew of the sea," rosemary grows best in France and Spain, where the fog rolls in from the Mediterranean. The leaves, which look like inch-long pine needles, are packaged "whole" and should be allowed to simmer about fifteen minutes to release their flavor in a recipe. A potent yet friendly herb, rosemary mixes well with other seasonings and is used frequently but sparingly in the cooking of lamb, chicken, shrimp, spoon bread, eggplant, turnips, cauliflower, green beans, beets, summer squash, and fruits.

SAFFRON
(Crocus sativus)

ONE-THIRD of all the recipes of well-to-do, ancient households called for saffron, the dried stigmas of an ancient member of the crocus family described as the world's most costly spice. Solomon, king of the Hebrews and husband of many wives, listed saffron as one of his favorite "garden delights." Henry VIII, "Defender of the Faith," was so fond of saffron in his viands that he forbade court ladies to use it for hair dye. Each *Crocus sativus* blossom yields but three delicate, orange-colored filaments (stigmas), which must be picked by hand. It takes more than 225,000 of them to make one pound. Luckily, a little saffron goes a long way. Saffron is highly valued as a distinctive scent in Oriental types of perfume and as a seasoning for many foods, especially in Spain. Use saffron to achieve a rich, golden color and exotic flavor in rolls, biscuits, and rice dishes. (Add a pinch of it to boiling water before adding rice.) *Arroz Con Pollo*, a noted Spanish chicken and rice dish, cannot be made without it.

SAGE
(*Salvia officinalis*)

SAGE, a hardy perennial of the mint family native to the Mediterranean area, was at the top of any medieval list of potherbs, grown mainly for "potage," salads, and meat pies. *The Goodman of Paris* describes how to season white wine with sage, ginger, and bay leaf, and how to ease a toothache by "breathing the steam of boiling water into which sage and other herbs have been set." Physicians at the great medical school of Salerno asked, "Why should a man die whilst sage grows in his garden?" Slender and green when picked, sage leaves turn to a silvery grey when dried. Use this herb in the cooking of pork and other meats, poultry stuffings, baked fish, salad dressings, and clam chowder. New Englanders serve sage cheese on Thanksgiving Day. Buy it "whole," "rubbed" (fine), or "ground."

SAVORY
(Satureia hortensis)

IN spite of its flavorful name and the fact that it has been known for centuries, this notable herb of the mint family has remained almost untouched by myth and superstition, finding uses mainly in foods and medicaments. Hippocrates, the ancient Greek physician, prescribed savory for bilious attacks. Fifteenth-century apothecaries used it in the making of cough medicine. Including it in a recipe for goose in *Forme of*

Cury (Cookery), published in 1780, Samuel Pegge says: "Take sage, parsley, hyssop, and savory, quinces, pears, garlic, and grapes, and fill the geese therewith; sew the hole that no grease come out, and roast it well." Summer savory (sometimes called Bohnenkraut or bean herb) is far more popular than the perennial winter variety whose leaves are less aromatic. Imported from France and Spain and used either "whole" or "ground," savory is an important ingredient in poultry seasoning and is, by itself, very good in meats, soups, salads, dressings, and sauces.

SESAME SEED
(*Sesamum indicum*)

SESAME, also called "benne," is one of the oldest herb and oil-seed crops, especially favored in the Orient, Near East, and Africa. Assyrian mythology has it that the gods drank sesame wine before they made the earth. Ancient Greek and Roman soldiers packed the seed for nourishment on long marches. The pearly-white seed, rarely more than one-eighth of an inch in length, comes from an herbaceous plant which grows healthily in Nicaragua, Ethiopia, Mexico, Guatemala, Salvador, California, and Texas. Sold "whole," it takes on a rich, toasted-nut flavor when baked atop rolls and bread. Important to remember: When not exposed to oven heat, sesame seed should be toasted before use. Try using it as a substitute for finely chopped almonds.

TARRAGON
(*Artemisia dracunculus*)

TARRAGON, indigenous to Siberia and cultivated in the United States, France, and Yugoslavia, seems to have been virtually unknown in medieval Europe. Ibn Baithar, a physician and botanist, who lived in Spain in the thirteenth century, wrote that "the tender tops (leaves) of tarragon were cooked with vegetables and that tarragon juice was used to flavor drinks." He also said that "it sweetened the breath, dulled the taste of bitter medicine, and put one to sleep." A member of the aster family with an aroma suggestive of anise, tarragon is more often thought

Tarragon

Cloves

Bay
Leaves

Mustard

of as an ingredient in tarragon vinegar, sauce Béarnaise, and sauce Tartare than as a season ing for sauces, salads, meats and tomato dishes. Sprinkle broiled chicken with finely minced tarragon before removing it from the oven.

THYME
(Thymus vulgaris)

"You smell of thyme" was one of the finest compliments one ancient Greek could pay to another. Pedanius Dioscorides, an Athenian physician and herbalist, said "being eaten with meat it (thyme) avails for the dull sighted. It is good instead of sauce for the use in health." Pliny advised the melancholy to stuff their "crying pillows" with the herb. The thyme-scented honey of Mt. Hymettus is still described as the "very best." A perennial plant of the mint family, thyme is produced in the United States, France, Spain, and Portugal and is used in the seasoning of clam and fish chowders, sauces, croquettes, creamed chipped beef, creamed chicken, and seafood dishes. Use thyme butter over creamed white onions, braised celery, asparagus, green beans, and eggplant. Thyme and fresh tomatoes go together like hand and glove.

TURMERIC
(*Curcuma longa*)

Best known in the United States as an ingredient in prepared mustard and mustard pickles, turmeric (sometimes called "tumeric") has been used for many other purposes, particularly to give the skin a golden glow. The aromatic root of an East Indian plant closely related to ginger, turmeric is one of the most important spices in curry powder and is used "ground" in chicken and egg dishes, creamed potatoes, rice, and macaroni. Add a dash of it to mayonnaise for seafood salads and to melted butter for corn-on-the-cob.

DEHYDRATED VEGETABLE SEASONINGS

Dehydrated vegetable seasonings, inspired by the age-old idea of drying food to preserve it, have become very popular with kitcheners, largely because of their no-fuss, no-muss con-

venience and storability. Useful in endless recipes, these flavorful additives should always be
at hand on your herb and spice shelf.

CELERY FLAKES

MAKE use of these palatable dehydrated, flaked
leaves and stalks of vegetable celery in soups,
stews, sauces, stuffings, and other dishes which
call for celery flavor. To soften flakes, add an
equal amount of water and let stand for ten
minutes.

GARLIC (*Allium sativum*)

VIEWED as a vegetable as well as an herb, garlic
has become an important adjunct to American
cooking, particularly since California producers
came up with a dehydration process whereby
it could be offered "pure" in two different, easy-
to-use types: Instant minced garlic and instant
garlic powder (granulated). A third choice, garlic salt, combines garlic powder with salt. Use
the minced variety in dishes which require
cooking, so that all of the true garlic flavor can
be released. Garlic powder and garlic salt sur-
render their flavors instantly, without cooking.

40

Mixed Vegetable Flakes

A MIXTURE of dehydrated, flaked onion, celery, green and red peppers, and carrot which provides a handy, rich seasoning for soups, stews, sauces, and stuffings. To soften flakes, add an equal amount of water and let stand for ten minutes.

Onion (*Allium cepa*)

THERE are some five hundred different kinds of onions. The California variety, low in moisture and high in flavor, is best suited to dehydration. Safe to say, there is a dehydrated *Allium cepa* for every occasion where onion flavor might be desired. More specifically: an instant onion powder (granulated) for dishes requiring no onion texture; instant minced or flaked onion for dishes requiring onion texture; instant toasted onion flakes for adding an additional flavor note; and, finally, onion salt, a combination of onion powder and salt.

Sweet Pepper Flakes

CHOOSE, as you wish, a mixture of dehydrated, flaked sweet green or red peppers, or a mixture of both green and red, the latter being sweet, not hot. Any one of the mixtures goes flavorfully in salads, sauces, vegetables, and casseroles. To soften flakes, add an equal amount of water and let stand for ten minutes.

BLENDS

Many blends, or mixtures, of herbs and spices have been developed to ease the art of cookery. In some cases, a specific blend may be unique with the company which packages it; in others, it may be a blend which has been adopted by most packagers. All in all, the blends listed here are sold by most firms and are available in food stores throughout the United States.

Apple Pie Spice

A blend of ground sweet baking spices, including clove, nutmeg or mace, allspice, and ginger, for use in all fruit pies and pastries.

Barbecue Spice

A blend of ground spices, such as chili pepper, cumin, garlic, clove, and paprika, designed to provide the basic seasoning for a barbecue sauce, but also good in salad dressings, meat casseroles, hash brown potatoes, eggs, and cheese dishes.

CHILI POWDER

CHILI powder, an American idea created about one hundred years ago for the seasoning of "Tex-Mex" dishes, is a blend of spices, consisting of chili pepper (the basic ingredient), ground cumin seed, oregano, powdered garlic — and sometimes ground clove, allspice, and powdered onion. Besides being the basic seasoning for Americanized Mexican dishes, such as chili con carne, chili powder is also good in shellfish and oyster cocktail sauces, scrambled eggs, hamburgers, gravies, and stews.

CINNAMON SUGAR

THERE are few, if any, times in cooking and baking when cinnamon is not accompanied by sugar; thus this skillful blend of the two should be a handy item to include on your herb and spice shelf. It is especially useful for cinnamon toast and as a quick topping for many other sweet goods. Try it on a slice of fresh white bread and butter!

CRAB BOIL OR SHRIMP SPICE

THESE blends, which may be similar or identical (depending on the manufacturer), are mixtures of whole spices, such as bay leaf, peppercorn, red pepper, mustard seed, and ginger, which should be added to the water when boiling seafood.

CURRY POWDER

A BLEND of sixteen to twenty ground spices designed to give dishes the characteristic flavor of Indian curry cookery. Undoubtedly the oldest of all spice blends, curry powder *per se* includes ginger, turmeric, fenugreek, clove, coriander, cumin seed, black pepper, red pepper, and others, depending on the manufacturer's formula. Apart from curry recipes, it is also used in vegetables, fish, meat, French dressing, scalloped tomatoes, clam and fish chowders, and split pea soup.

Cinnamon

Anise

Sage

Celery Seed

HERB SEASONING

ESPECIALLY suited to salads and salad dressings, this blend varies somewhat according to the brand, but the end uses are essentially the same. Keep in mind that the term "herb" refers specifically to the milder-flavored leafy seasonings (i.e., marjoram, oregano, basil, chervil, etc.) as opposed to the stronger-flavored spices (i.e., pepper, clove, cinnamon, etc.).

ITALIAN SEASONING

CREATED in response to the growing demand for pizza and pasta dishes, this blend of herbs and spices, satisfying most but not all taste requirements, is certainly typical of many Italian creations, containing oregano, basil, red pepper, rosemary, and possibly garlic powder.

MIXED PICKLING SPICE

THIS blend, used by good cooks since the turn of the century, includes whole spices, such as mustard seed, black and white peppercorns, bay leaf, dill seed, red pepper, ginger, cinnamon, mace, allspice, coriander seed, and others. It is used for pickling and preserving meats, and for seasoning vegetables, stews, soups, sauces, and relishes.

POULTRY SEASONING

A BLEND of ground herbs, including sage, thyme, marjoram, savory, and sometimes rosemary, for use in poultry, pork, veal, and fish stuffings. It also goes well with paprika in meat loaf and in biscuit batter served with chicken or turkey.

PUMPKIN PIE SPICE

ALTHOUGH it was designed primarily for pumpkin pie, this blend of ground cinnamon, nutmeg, clove, and ginger is also good in spice cookies, gingerbread, and breakfast buns. For a delicious "something new," French fry slices of raw pumpkin, and dust with pumpkin pie spice.

SEAFOOD SEASONING

THIS ground blend, widely used in seafood sauces, contains approximately the same items found in Crab Boil or Shrimp Spice, with salt added.

Seasoned or Flavored Salt

A mixture of herbs, spices, and salt, this all-purpose seasoning goes by different names according to the brand. Many restaurants use it in cooking and place it next to pepper on tables. It is well suited to meats, vegetables, sauces, and dairy foods.

Other Blends

Besides those mentioned here, there are numerous other blends of herbs and spices which are offered by one manufacturer or another. It has been said, and it could be true, that there is a specific blend for nearly every recipe that ever appeared in a cookbook. There are, for example, blends for ham, roast beef, hamburger, veal, chicken, lamb, pork, and fish; for vegetables in general, and for mashed potatoes in particular; for salads and dressings; for eggs, pasta dishes, and gravies; for sweet doughs, pies, cakes, and many, many more.

Pray tell, with so many seasonings to choose from, how could any dish be dull?

Try Your Hand With Herbs and Spices

A PROPER herb and spice shelf could contain upwards of one hundred different seasonings. To be practical, you might start by familiarizing yourself with those which good cooks use most often in the preparation of everyday recipes; namely, black pepper, cinnamon, nutmeg, garlic salt or powder, paprika, chili powder, mace, oregano, celery salt or seed, onion salt or powder, parsley flakes, poultry seasoning, mixed pickling spice, clove, bay leaf, dry (seed or powdered) mustard, red pepper, sage, allspice, and ginger. It is hoped that the following recipes will prove helpful in your introduction to herbs and spices.

HERB AND SPICE RECIPES
APPETIZERS

PARTY CHEESE FINGERS

MIX ground white pepper, instant garlic powder, and onion salt with a 3-oz. package of cream cheese. Spread over slices of bread, cut into finger strips, and top each with a strip of dill pickle or thinly sliced cucumber. Makes 12 fingers.

Toasted Paprika Crackers

Spread thin crackers with butter or margarine. Sprinkle lightly with paprika, and place under broiler to brown. Serve with soup or salad.

Orange-Mace Spread

Combine a 3-oz. package of cream cheese, 1/3 cup drained, diced fresh oranges, 2 teaspoons fresh lemon juice, and ½ teaspoon ground mace. Serve on squares of toast. Makes 16 squares.

Chili Cheese Fingers

Blend ½ cup grated, sharp Cheddar cheese with ¼ cup (½ stick) butter or margarine, and 1 teaspoon chili powder. Trim crusts from 8 slices of bread and toast only on one side. Spread untoasted side with chili-cheese mixture, and cut each slice into 4 fingers. Arrange on baking sheet, and place under broiler to brown. Serve with salad. Makes 32 fingers.

English Rabbit Canapés

Cut 6 slices of bread into 1½-inch squares. Sauté one side in 2 or 3 tablespoons of butter or margarine, and toast the other side. Combine 1 cup (¼ pound) grated, sharp American cheese, ⅛ teaspoon black pepper, ¼ teaspoon powdered mustard, and 4 teaspoons sherry. Spread over toasted sides of bread slices. Broil about 1 minute or until cheese is melted and golden brown. Serve hot, garnished with parsley flakes. Makes 24 canapés.

Fish Dishes

Parsley Broiled Fish

Melt 1/3 cup of butter or margarine in a saucepan. Add 1½ teaspoons parsley flakes, ½ teaspoon salt, and 1½ teaspoons fresh lemon juice. Place 3 pounds of fish (cut 1-inch thick) in melted shortening and turn to coat both sides well. Place on a cold broiler rack. Broil for 7 minutes, turn, and continue broiling until done (approximately 5 minutes). Serve with parsley butter. Makes 6 servings.

Pepper

Rosemary

Nutmeg

Caraway

Herbed Oven-fried Fish

Wash and clean 6 small fish (whole). Combine ½ cup pancake mix, ½ teaspoon crumbled oregano leaves, 2 teaspoons salt, and ¼ teaspoon ground black pepper. Add fish and shake well to coat with mixture. In the meantime, heat ¼ cup of shortening in a 12x9x2-inch baking pan in a preheated oven (400°F.). Add fish and bake for 20 minutes. Turn and bake until brown on other side (about 20 minutes). Makes 6 servings. This is a delicious main course for luncheon or dinner.

Marinated Swordfish Steaks

Combine 1½ teaspoons salt, 2 teaspoons curry powder, 1/3 cup salad oil, 1 tablespoon fresh lemon juice, and 1 tablespoon cider vinegar. Cut 2 pounds swordfish steaks into serving-size pieces. Add to marinade and let stand 5 to 6 hours. When ready to cook, remove fish from marinade, drain, and cook under a broiler until brown and flaky (15 to 20 minutes), basting with marinade left in pan. Makes 4 generous servings.

Meat Dishes

Curried Lamb Burgers

Shape 1 pound of ground, lean lamb into 4 patties, ½-inch thick. Sprinkle both sides with onion and garlic salts. Cook under broiler until brown (15 to 20 minutes), turning frequently. In the meantime, combine ¼ cup softened butter or margarine with ½ to ¾ teaspoon curry powder, and spread generously over both sides of cooked patties. Serve between hot hamburger buns. Makes 4 servings.

Veal Paprika

Soften ¼ cup of onion flakes in 3 tablespoons of water. Cut 2 pounds of boneless veal stew meat into 1-inch cubes, and brown in 2 tablespoons of shortening. Add softened onion. Stir and cook 2 to 3 minutes. Add 1 tablespoon paprika, 1¼ teaspoons salt, 1/16 teaspoon ground red pepper, 1 cup canned tomatoes, and ½ cup water or stock. Cover and cook 1 hour or until veal is tender. Add ½ cup sour cream just before serving. Serve with rice. Makes 6 servings.

Ham Steak Hawaiian

Brown 6 boneless ham steaks on both sides and place in baking dish. Remove skins from 3 medium, boiled sweet potatoes; cut in half and place over meat. Top with 6 pineapple sticks. Add 1/4 cup hot water to the drippings from browning the ham and pour over dish. Cover and bake in a preheated, moderate oven (350°F.) for 30 minutes. Peel 3 bananas, cut and arrange over top of pineapple. Sprinkle with 1 tablespoon brown sugar mixed with 1/2 teaspoon allspice. Dot with butter or margarine and brown under broiler. Makes 6 servings.

Caraway Sauerkraut with Pork Butts

Cook 2 pounds of lean pork butts in 2 inches of boiling water, along with 1 bay leaf and 1/4 teaspoon whole black pepper, for 45 minutes or until meat is tender. Remove pork butts and add 2 pounds of sauerkraut and 2 tablespoons caraway seed. Stir in 1/4 cup brown sugar and 2 cups diced tart apples. Cover and cook for 15 minutes. Serve hot with pork butts. Makes 6 to 8 servings.

Santa Fe Chili

Brown 1 pound of ground beef in 1 tablespoon of shortening. Soften 2 tablespoons instant minced onion in 2 tablespoons water. Add to the meat and brown. Stir in one can (10½-ozs.) tomato soup, 4 teaspoons chili powder, 2 teaspoons salt, ⅛ teaspoon ground black pepper, ½ teaspoon tarragon leaves, one No. 2 can (1-lb.) red kidney beans and a dash of ground red pepper. Heat thoroughly. Makes 4 servings.

Cumin Beef Patties

Combine 1½ pounds of ground chuck beef, 1 tablespoon minced onion, 1½ teaspoons salt, ¾ teaspoon ground cumin seed, ¼ teaspoon ground black pepper, and ⅛ teaspoon garlic powder. Shape into 6 patties ½-inch thick. Brown on both sides in a skillet over medium heat until done. Makes 6 servings.

Party Ideas

Zippy Cream Cheese Dip

Mash a 3-oz. package of cream cheese until smooth. Add ¼ cup catsup, ½ teaspoon onion

Saffron

Sesame
Seed

Marjoram

Red
Pepper

salt, ¼ teaspoon ground black pepper, ⅛ teaspoon garlic powder, and ¼ cup cream. Mix well. Place in a bowl and sprinkle with paprika. Surround with potato chips or fresh vegetable sticks, such as carrots, celery, or cucumbers. Makes ¾ cup.

Low Calorie Dip

Beat creamy cottage cheese in beater or blender until it has the consistency of sour cream. Add ground white pepper, instant minced onion, and instant garlic powder to taste. Garnish with paprika, and serve with fresh vegetable sticks or melon strips.

Onion Cocktail Dip

Soften a 3-oz. package of cream cheese with 2 tablespoons milk. Add 2 teaspoons instant minced onion, ½ teaspoon salt, ⅛ teaspoon garlic powder, and 1/16 teaspoon ground white pepper. Mix well. Serve in a small dish surrounded with crackers, potato chips, and fresh vegetable sticks. Makes 2/3 cup.

Paprika Sour Cream Dip

COMBINE 1 cup of sour cream, ⅛ teaspoon garlic powder, ½ teaspoon onion powder, 1/16 teaspoon cayenne, ¾ teaspoon salt, 2 tablespoons crumbled blue cheese, and ¾ teaspoon paprika. Place in a small bowl. Garnish with paprika, and serve with vegetable sticks and crackers. Makes 1 cup.

Quick Party Dip

FOR an exotic, quick-to-make dip, season mashed avocado with fresh lemon juice, chili powder, finely diced tomato, salt, and ground black pepper to taste. Garnish with paprika, and serve with potato chips or crackers.

SOUPS

Jiffy Herbed Vichyssoise

COMBINE a 10¼-oz. can of frozen cream of potato soup and a 10¾-oz. can of onion soup (not frozen). Dissolve 1 chicken bouillon cube in 2 cups of boiling water and add to soups. Stir in 1 tablespoon of parsley flakes, ¼ teaspoon ground white pepper and 1 cup heavy cream.

Heat only until hot enough to blend the flavors. Serve hot or chilled with instant minced onion and parsley flakes (¼ teaspoon each) sprinkled over the top of each portion. Makes 6 servings.

Chilled Tomato Soup

Combine a 10½-oz. can of tomato soup with equal amount of buttermilk, 1 tablespoon fresh lemon juice, ¼ teaspoon salt, 1/16 teaspoon instant garlic powder, ¼ teaspoon onion powder, and 2 teaspoons parsley flakes. Mix well and serve chilled. Makes 3 to 4 servings.

Caraway Soup

Simmer 3 tablespoons caraway seed in 3 cups of water for 10 minutes. Strain and discard the seed. Add 3 bouillon cubes. Brown 3 tablespoons fine dry bread crumbs lightly in 2 tablespoons butter, and sprinkle over top. Season to taste with a dash of instant garlic powder. Serves 4.

Vegetable Dishes
Lima Beans in Sour Cream

Cook one 10-oz. package frozen lima beans as directed on package. Remove from heat and stir in ½ cup sour cream, blended with ⅛ teaspoon ground cumin seed and 1/16 teaspoon ground black pepper. Serve at once. Makes 4 servings.

FRESH GINGERED CARROTS

COMBINE 1 tablespoon fresh lemon juice, 1 teaspoon salt, 1 teaspoon sugar, ¾ teaspoon ground ginger, and ⅛ teaspoon ground black pepper. Sprinkle over 1½ pounds sliced cooked carrots. Dot with butter or margarine and bake in a preheated oven (400°F.) for 45 minutes. Makes 6 servings.

CORN AU GRATIN

MIX together 3 cups whole kernel corn, ½ cup medium white sauce, ½ cup shredded sharp American cheese, 1 teaspoon salt, ¼ teaspoon ground white pepper, and 1½ teaspoons paprika. Turn into a 1-quart casserole. Melt 2 tablespoons butter or margarine. Add ½ cup soft bread crumbs and mix well. Sprinkle over casserole. Bake in a preheated moderate oven (350°F.) for 25 minutes or until crumbs are browned. Makes 4 servings.

Fresh Snap Beans with Basil Butter

Melt 3 tablespoons of butter or margarine. Stir and cook until dark brown. Add 2 teaspoons fresh lemon juice, ¼ teaspoon salt, 1/16 teaspoon ground black pepper, and ½ teaspoon crumbled basil leaf. Toss lightly with 1 pound of hot cooked fresh snap beans. Makes 4 servings.

Spiced Beets

Add to a saucepan 1/3 cup cider vinegar, 1/3 cup juice drained from one can of beets, 1 tablespoon sugar, and ⅛ teaspoon garlic powder. Add 1 tablespoon mixed pickling spice tied in a cheese cloth bag. Bring to boiling point, and pour over beets. Cool. Chill and serve as an accompaniment to meat or fish. Makes 2 cups.

In *Physiologie du Goût*, Brillat-Savarin says: "The discovery of a new dish does more for human happiness than the discovery of a new star."
